AF413307

The Desultory Thoughts of Two Traveling Brothers

The Desultory Thoughts of Two Traveling Brothers

AMBROSE and ZEBULON BURKE

RESOURCE *Publications* · Eugene, Oregon

THE DESULTORY THOUGHTS OF TWO TRAVELING BROTHERS

Resource Publications
An Imprint of Wipf and Stock Publishers
199 W. 8th Ave., Suite 3
Eugene, OR 97401

www.wipfandstock.com

PAPERBACK ISBN: 979-8-3852-0748-0
HARDCOVER ISBN: 979-8-3852-0749-7
EBOOK ISBN: 979-8-3852-0750-3

12/05/23

To Grandma and Pop Burke,
Who have been the rock upon which we have flourished
And to Grandma and Pop Dunn,
Whose work ethic has inspired us greatly

Contents

Comfort in the Chaos *by Ambrose*

How strange it is
To be surrounded by so many
yet to still feel so alone.
They are best friends and coworkers;
They are family and classmates;
They are teammates and acquaintances.
But I do not tell them

I know I should, but I don't
So much to say and so few ways to say it phrase
I know I won't be ridiculed
I won't be shunned or rejected
Yet for some reason, I stay closed
Tighter than the bundles I wrap myself in at night
The ones that keep me warm
The ones that keep everything inside,
Never to be let out

But what to say, what to say!
Why is it so hard?
I do this to no one but myself
I listen to other people
I give them advice
I give them a personal confidant
I'm no martyr for this, not even close
I do it because I like to
But to have others listen to me?
I would rather talk to my blade

And now it comes to this:
I sit in my dark crevice and write
Not out of love, or some unrealized genius
But out of frustration
Out of jealousy
Out of fear
I pretend I'm Poe, or Yates, or the next Shakespeare
But I'm not.
I am a sad, sullen creature
With no doctor to have borne me this burden
So that I may point and say
"Here lies the true monster!"

Why have I come to this desolate waste?
Have I come seeking wisdom, or fortune?
Perhaps I seek to inspire, or to relate?
No, I come because of greed.
I want what others have.
I want it for myself, and I want them to have nothing
I want not sympathy for this nor for anything
I want a million things besides
But I know it will not happen

For who deserves such rewards?
Not I
Not I who has transgressed,
And transgressed again,
And again,
And again once more.
Conceit and ego demand that I,
Who is as fallible as any, and then more,
Think that I should deserve what they have
And I see that notion and laugh (add period if wanted)

Such things go to those who were born with them
Not that I have not been,
But just that I have squandered them without realizing.
Quite the nerve,
To suggest that I myself am still the victim,
When my abuser is my reflection,
And still think I need,
No, deserve!
What they have

I write not for sympathy,
Or retribution,
Or glory,
But for jealousy.
For greed.
And for myself.

Summers End *by Zebulon*

Summer is the coasting season
Following a spring where life blooms
To the summer high of happiness
Which is followed by autumns gloom

It's a time where the days are filled
Of friends, shorelines, and fishing
And long nights of fireworks and stars
And the firefly bugs of lightning

It's on the final day of summer
Sitting along the shore alone
The crisp air gains a slight chill
For the season's shift in tone

One can only reminisce
Of the summer joy that's made
From campfires to swimming to all
For despair was just a charade

Summers end is growing old
A season for children and teens
Where joy is pure and lively
For adulthood makes it unseen

The lowly air reminds us to grow
That the sunshine will cease to be
The sanguine light of innocence
Growing old makes hard to see

Only in your own young children
Will summers joy reignite
And remind you of all you had
After every summers night

It's always sad to see it go
To feel the melancholy change
From the warm embracing air of summer
To a colder, somnolent autumn mange

Take your time to sit and still
To rejoice as the sound of waves crash on
To remember the joyous summer now at end
To reminisce the memories you've gifted upon

Concerns Due to Customers *by Ambrose*

You don't know me.
Most likely, you never will.
And if you're lucky,
You won't begin to feel the way I do

I'm no Dolly Parton,
But I work my nine-to-five.
I clear tables, I run food, I tease my coworkers.
And every once in a while, I ogle at the odd customer.

Frankly, it was a lousy shift (insert period but not needed if it's a stylistic choice)
It was long, arduous, and annoying
You guys made my job difficult.
Yet here I am, coveting your time there

I was fine until I wasn't
Until I pushed her towards you
Until I made her do what I couldn't;
Just talking to you seems impossible

I love her for who she is to me
But I despise her for who she is to you
I know I'll never be her to you,
But here I am regardless

I wish you hadn't come in
I wish you didn't make her happy
I wish you two didn't meet
I wish you all the best

Please, go on with your life and never read this
It's better you don't know my pathetic ramblings
Of a boy too cowardly to go after something
No matter how much he wants it

I hope we never meet,
It's better for both of us if we don't
And I hope I never feel this way again.
Because I'm not sure I'll make it through

I don't know you
But I know what you represent.
You represent everything I want
And everything I'll never have.

Past Emanations *by Zebulon*

I sit here under the stars
Listening on to the music
Played just in my own world
Of the apartment started by both
A young man and a girl
Marked by address 1142k
Where the latter left
And the former stayed
And all he has left now is
The music of his regifted self
Where his own world emanates
Through lyrics and melodies of the old

As cigar smoke lingers
And the night stars watch on
As he tries to encompass who he was
When he was in his own little world
But here he sits in a world too familiar
But not close enough
Out on his parents lawn he sits
Where his old self still rules
But has detached from his new old
Where the man of 1142k once ruled
Now has disappeared back
And he is now lost

His writing has faltered
His emotions have drained
A stoicism all but lost
To where has he gone
But past emanations of 1142k?
Come back I urge you, come back

To my Best Friend *by Ambrose*

I'm sorry I'm not always there for you
Even when I should be
And when I'm there, I'm not really *there*
I can't always give you the advice you wanna hear,
But just know that it's what I think you need to
I won't always be able to be there
But I'll try.

I won't lie to you
And I know that makes me seem abrasive
But I never liked her
It should have been a hint
That no one else did either
But you love her now
And for you, my brother
I can love her as a sister

I never hated you
Not even when you called me that word
Not when I slapped you
And not even when you refused to listen
I can never stay mad
And I hope the same is true for you

Just know that through my failings and faults,
My misdeeds and misgivings,
That I do care for you
And I will sweat and fight and die for you
Until my last breath

My dear beloved friend,
I can't always say how I feel
I probably never will be able to
So I write this now
Knowing you won't read it
But hoping that you'll feel it
And when we're together at the end
I think we'll be living it.

I Want You, at the Cost of You *by Zebulon*

Beautiful eyes, so green and true
Drowning my once sad ocean of blue
I want you now, to take you away
But will I make you wither and decay?
A desire so strong, to have it go through
But to be with me, will it cost you, You?

Anthony *by Ambrose*

And why, I ask, do I give my affection to you?
if Not to be returned, then for what?
there are Thousands of people out there
and yet you Have my attention alone
if it meant having Only you, I would do just about anything
but here I stay, a Nile's distance away,
jealous of those who can keep You close

Irascible Cognizance *by Zebulon*

Time ceases to exist
As does any reality,
The world becomes nothing more
Than a creation to be destroyed.

The humanity begins to leave
And what's left behind is automation
For which a user has lost control
Like a program running itself
As the muscles begin to tense
And feelings have given up to one

You begin to look around
What can break, what will break
What can I begin to break
What makes the loudest sound
It must make a sound
It's the sound that satisfies the urge

The mind has lost all meaning
For a millenniums worth of growth has gone
All the progress, dissipating leaving a light feel
Where physical limitations cannot occur
What is heavy is light, what is light is air

But the object must break
An unbreakable object satisfies no mind
A mind where destruction has taken over
It must shatter, not crack
To become unrecognizable, not scratched

Feeling it in your hands reality pounces
If only for a second will it catch up
Is this right? Where am I?
No! The urge must be satisfied!
I can't break this! Who will I be?
You will be a time bomb still! Destroy!
I'll be a slave to Desire, control!
Shatter!
No!
Then you are weak!
Am I?

Time has ceased still
Sound has not registered
For the senses have ran in fear
Of the beast that emerged from within
Touch is all to remain
One must feel the object in hand

Many moments define a man
And we are nothing but small children
With many molds of ourselves overgrown
As the child is pushed deeper in
As our years push past us
Becoming more of the demon it can be
Waiting to become re-emerged
At the slightest spilling of milk
Or the common drop of a glass
For the demon is trapped in us
But will wield any power it takes

The world is still stopped
For this moment will define us
Will this object shatter?
Will it be saved ?
Shatter!
No!
Control!

I wish I was Erin *by Ambrose*

I wish I was Erin
Not in name,
Or body,
Or spirit,
Or mind,
But in life
In *his* life

Oh, to be Erin
To have that time alone with him
To be the one he wants
To be anything to him
Is to be fulfilled

Alas, I am not Erin
I am not the one he looks at
I am not the one he talks to
I am not anyone or anything to him
And I never will be

I am not Erin
But I really wish I was

The Heart of a Dead Friend *by Zebulon*

I see the pain in your eyes
Although it seems to be remnants
Of the pain once felt
For it has long since moved
Into a certain death, not of nature
But of neglect
For the most painful way to go
Is not from hatred
But one of indifference

Perhaps the only living pain
Was the one in my heart
For the one in yours was already gone
And I sat there
Lost in my mind
For who was I to be?
How is a friend to act?
Does he embrace ?
Or shall he just listen
For all the answers in the world
Might not be enough
As the hardest solutions to find
Are the ones I'm not meant to find for you

Again, for what does that make me?
I cannot ask as Freud.
Nor speak like Whitman
Or engage as Petersen
Even feel the heartbreak of Solzhenitsyn
For those minds aren't mine

And to try and be them
Gets me lost in my own
Like cigar smoke lost in the air

How can one speak?
To feel pain that only the one can truly know?
I couldn't do enough
But sit and listen on
To portray someone I am not
Sitting your heart decays
As the corpse it already is

I have failed you as a friend
Or what one should be
To solve? To listen? To guide?
For what have I done
But all except all three
Because a Jack of all trades
Is but a master of none
Where mastery is needed

For you I can only feel the pain
As the emanation it is
Or what it's perceived to be
While you must take the journey alone
As I watch from afar
But the pain from the dead
Is far different than the one of the coroner
Who views the body as a specimen
Never finding a cure
And only coming across the body
As it lays there in lifeless remorse

I wish I could've done more
Or perhaps it was too late
But it was not enough

It can never be enough
It will never be enough
To my friend, to a best friend
I have failed you
And I'm sorry
I have failed.

Pop *by Ambrose*

Today was a first day:
There are many firsts, some of them days
But today was one of the important firsts

Yesterday, Dad said his first thought was you
When he learned of the scrimmage, he thought,
Perhaps he would take you there to watch
But you are not there, not anymore,
And you were yesterday, but today is today

The stands on Friday nights will be full
But they'll still feel empty
No crowd can fill the space you left
And although you're watching
In that great stadium in the sky,
I wish you were still watching down here

A moment of silence isn't enough,
To replace the silence that
Took us when you left
The roar of the crowd
Will sound about as loud
As the wings of a cardinal

$5 for a ticket
But you get in for free
The cost is still paid,
For us, for me
And for everyone else who knew you

You were always more than you thought,
Grandpa
And you'll always mean more to me
Than you'll ever know

Mourning A Nondeath *by Zebulon*

I gaze upon the photos
For which I have left
Then the videos
To hear it all again
To remember once a better day
Before our life went away

For how do you mourn a Non-Death?
Of someone who made you alive
To whom was your world
Before she moved onto her next?

How can one cope with death
Not of a life but a past
Where her soul walks the earth
But is no longer yours
Where four footprints became two
Before she found another pair

You become aimlessly wandering
What happened? To what has become?
A whole life now a distant memory
Any glimpse of the life past you retain
Now has become a whole
Of what was once supplementary.

You might be alone
But you cannot go back
She occupied it once
A book you already read,
Why expect another end?

It was a boy and a girl
Where she was the same path
Until she turned left,
And you, right
For the middle rock
Became a dividing fork,

But this isn't time to rewind
On a road with one direction
On hers she found another man
Perhaps you another girl
But the memory still stands
And in memory you grieve

But to mourn a living, a non-death
Of a girl you once had
Knowing it to be the ultimate end
Of a girl still alive who died.

Struggles with Substances *by Ambrose*

Drug of my heart,
Used willingly for too long
I am now forced to cut myself off
But I struggle to find a reason to do so

Liquor of my thoughts,
It's taste is sweeter than any wine
But I'm never ready for the hangover
Even when I drank it regularly
No intervention could sober me
And any other alcohol won't taste the same

Medicine of my soul,
Once saved me, now plagues me
I used to need to live,
But now the cure is worse than the disease
No doctor or nurse can save
What little remains of my withered person

Cigarette of my essence,
Its very scent captivates me
The flavor is too addictive
Any other form is too weak to satiate
Or maybe, I am too weak to resist

Cure of my being,
I look for it still
I see it, in the distance
A mountain ways up,
An oceans length away,

But still attainable, conceivable
Reachable

Until I reach it, I remain a slave
A slave to the cigarette,
To the medicine and the liquor,
And a slave to the drug

1142k *by Zebulon*

There was a corner of a world
It was my corner
It was my rebirth
It was called 1142k

It was in a distant July we began
Back when life was sorted
Her and I began a new life
Which stemmed out of the old
Our laughs were shared in those walls
Ambitions, dreams, futures too
Love in both making and words
For it was our corner first

The walls of the corner witnessed
The lies and deceit of it all
The destruction and crumble
Where two became one
And what was once shared
Was now left by the one
And remained with the other

And to that did life sort again
Creating from the downfall
A new man, from his old self
Indistinguishable from his old
In all but his heart and eyes
Which reflect but the pain
Of the story in which no one knew
But the corners of his world alone

For from Rome's fall came a new life
Where the Renaissance came but later
And as such did the old new
Came the newer new

He took to his written words
Words reflected from his heart
He wrote for no one except him
He lived for none other but him
Witnessed and watched by no being
All except for God himself
Who in all his grace granted this pain
To have him reborn to be a new

And for months this new man lived
He lived in pain and love
He discovered, he learned anew
And lived a life in none other
Than life's own serendipity
And his own equanimity

But to what has happened to him now
For he lost his own corner
And returned to one of the older old
From where he grew before 1142k
But that's now where he remains
Where his old and new self fight
For what was built in one place
Will certainly falter in another

His soul was refined in 1142k
And for now it wanders where it can
Finding a purpose and a new life
A new enigma, a being to be
But all he lives in now is a shadow
Of who he was just briefly in time

In a corner of the world
Which was his rebirth
Which was my rebirth
It was his 1142k,
It was our 1142k,
It was my 1142k.
It was my own corner of the world
Called none other than 1142k.

Ouroboros *by Ambrose*

Why does the snake bite its own tail?
Surely it knows it cannot be good for it
For even if it loves the sensation,
It is still hurting itself

The tail taunts the snake, drawing it ever nearer
By being flamboyant and intoxicating
Until the snake's head has to lash out
The tail never enjoys the bite, but it loves the chase

The snake cannot control itself around the tail
It needs to bite the tail just as much as the tail needs to be bit,
No matter how much it knows it will regret it
No tail is ever worth the chase, and no chase is ever worth the bite

Taking a Chance at Failure *by Zebulon*

I lost myself so long ago
Like in the book Archipelago
Drifting away by tears held back
A river not flawed, ready to crack
Will she be my heart, my soul, my life?
Or just another lie, a time, a strife?

Final Departure *by Ambrose*

Still you have yet to leave
I can see you standing just across the way
And yet,
I am a world and a half removed
The rivers and valleys that separate us
With nothing to help me cross it
So here I will stand,
And there you will go
Undeterred by the world and a half before you

Ineffable Hatred *by Zebulon*

Where does one seek to go,
When the one you know is your own foe?
For you yourself, a lover a friend,
But only to myself I cannot make an amend.

Perhaps its by knowing yourself the best
A marker, you use it to judge the rest.
You with all your selfish greed,
Looking at all the good you need.

The only heart you know is your own
Where a humans real true evil is shown
A men of degeneracy, small and weak
Paints a picture oh so bleak.

If another being of evil takes shape,
At least in yourself you may escape
But if the one to turn is in your skin
How hard it is to ignore your sin?

They say its yourself that you must love
From friends to wives, you place above
But its in the mirror I see who I hate,
Where mercy and grace will have to wait.

To many others, my intentions may shy
But my wicked heart has certainly lied
And sinned so much I can't repent
For much of it was reckless intent

SO why trust others? For I look within
And I see no go, it's the wicked to win
Throw me in the fire, to the lions pit
For it is your love I am unfit

But lest we forget, they are not we
And although they contain bad we cannot see
They contain all the good that's in a heart
And its love in which is the larger part.

Broken Rose *by Ambrose*

Is the value of the broken rose
Measured in what it once was?
A perfect, vibrant organism
Flawless and beautiful
Flourishing in its garden
Now broken and ravaged,
Its petals lie crushed and withered
And the color which made it so beautiful
Has faded

But maybe there's a beauty in the broken
A reminder of what once was
Or,
A realization that maybe it wasn't so perfect
Maybe those petals weren't always so crisp
It's color, not always so vibrant
But what was once good can still be good
Even it's thorns,
Dangerous and sharp,
Still hold a beauty not unknown
And even when those thorns fall to the earth
It will bring a new broken perfection to the world

Love that Lasts *by Zebulon*

I want a love in transcendence.
Not of a time or place, but plane
Through us, through Him, in Him
By God, Through us, With us,
An exhibition of beauty seen nowhere
But our hearts, our soul, forever entailed.

Starlove *by Ambrose*

I think that the most beautiful thing
About the stars
Is that
Everyone who's ever loved
Across all of time and history
Has looked up at those same stars
Meaning that the thousands of stars in the sky
Are all full of love
A love that no distance can change
Because eventually,
We all see the same stars

So if the stars can be full of love
Maybe we can be, too

Pernicious, Stigmatized, and Rationally Irrational *by Zebulon*

No other name does carry
The stigma of a feeling
That one feels with another
When feelings are rather reeling

Jealousy is not an irrational foe
Coming across with immature style
But rather a genuine impetuous
A feeling with so much vile

Consider it not a prevention to other
But one that longs to be
For we wish to be around you
And be all that you can see

One of jealousy does not restrict
For we wish to see you free
But just take us along for a ride
And experience with you the glee

The fear is not to see you happy
But rather to see you forget
The reason you keep us around
A happiness we try to beget

What if you forget about us
And the happy times we had
Of the movie nights and singing
For we wish to see you glad

Men like me wonder the earth
Seeing you in all we view
For you are always on our minds
Dreaming of memories on constant cue

Maybe one day you be alone
And realize we are not enough
Or find another to take our place
To take you through life's rough

Forgive us if we seem at Ill ease
For it's a hard feeling to elucidate
How can we describe it to you?
Most others just become irate

We just wish to see you happy
But a happiness to be with us
And not to go through life alone,
Or with another on life's bus

So we must remain in silence
To suffer in our own measly mind
For no matter how we might seem to you
It's to ourselves we are the most unkind.

My Lady Jealousy *by Ambrose*

My dear, beloved Lady,
Whom I envy above all else,
Is not a vindictive creature.
My Lady is sweet, innocent, and kind
She cares for me, and I for her,
And she harbors no resentment.

It is not her character, but her nature that I envy
That I so desperately desire
For she acquires so easily that which I cannot have

It is not her fault for being so pure,
So beautiful and seductive,
Yet I blame her still

Her looks grab his attention
Where my words would simply fail me
And her eyes stare deep into places I could only dream of

Jealousy overtakes me
Constantly, she tears away at my soul
Until I am left with nothing but rage and envy

Her voice soothes the souls of men
Where my presence would only disturb
But she realizes not what she is doing

My Lady, so blissful and loving,
I ask of you only to gran me mercy and forgiveness
As I can only give to you in return my envy

The Love and Her Shore *by Zebulon*

The end of the earth it's called
Or of the end land where we stand
Where one can face out towards the blue
With all of God's landlocked beauty behind

You see, God exhibits his land creations
With rivers and streams which flow
And mountains to soar above
Of which he let man reside
To cast a harmony through the woods
Which in a green or a snow color
To shed the joy of his vision

But to go where it all ends
To sit out and stare in awe
Where the land and it's end meets
In a harmony of sand and sea
As the foam scurries itself up
And the land is washed away
As if both desire to be together
Or to be one of the same

The end of the earth, the shore
Exhibits not the final end
But the culmination of it all
With the endless accounts of all nature
So complexly interlocked
But also beautifully displayed
As no other physical being can replicate

To some it's the end, to me it's the shore
With it's never ending sight which lies ahead
But it's from standing on the loose ground
In which she is cemented in my mind

For God put all his woman on the land
And in particular there is one
Who's heart belongs along the sandy shore
While another heart belongs to her

I can stare in awe at the shore
But even then are my eyes on her
As her eyes reflect on the waves
As she looks upon the harmonic beauty
Are mine locked into her
For although God created this end
To be looked in utter serenity
Does he lest forget his other creation
For which in her lies a life ahead
As I look on upon to her
With all of a life behind

For God can create his end
And the creations to and from
But I'll always look onto mine
As they reflect not the end of the earth
But the end of a world I call Her.

Freedom Soon Regained *by Ambrose*

Could it finally be?
Is the dark storm finally dispersed by
The breaking of your dawn's light?
Are you the dove returning with the olive branch?

Far too long I've been trapped
Held in my endless maze
By one who would not so much as look my way
Now you come into my life
Leading the way out
Better than any golden string

I'm not out yet, not completely
My Odyssey has a few more chapters
But the battle has been fought
And the journey home begun
With you as my guide
I can't imagine going back.

Quixotic Loves *by Zebulon*

A love so perfect
Only a writer can write it
A love so pure
Only a Heart has felt it.

Amor Est *by Ambrose*

Love is the penny found by a young child
It is new, interesting, excitable
Worthy of a moments notice
Pouring more emotion into it than anything
It has a greater value now then it will later
And the penny is suddenly rarer than diamond
And just as long lasting

Love is the pillow lied on every night
Close, comforting, and familiar
It's presence, soothing
It's longevity is its worth
Simply being there every time is enough to satisfy
Whilst similar, each pillow differs
Some are stiff, others soft
But people have preferences and are discovering them
And much unlike the penny, the pillow's value wanes

Love is the heirloom sitting in the china cabinet
Unappreciated at first,
But upon reexamination,
Becomes a hoard of riches
So beautiful, but equally fragile
Lasting for some but shattering for others
Unique in its appearance, similar in its function
Projecting onto the next generation
A story or lesson

Love is the old man sitting on the park bench
Alone, sullen, and ancient
A warning of what could be
A reminder of what once was
For the old man had waited for love to find him
Like he once found that penny
Or slept on that pillow
And broke that heirloom
Instead of looking for a nickel
Getting a new pillow
And cherishing that heirloom

Love is the grave, so tenderly cared for
A mark of those who will never forget

Little Did I Know *by Zebulon*

It was many years ago, before today
When she came to class and looked my way
A girl unknown, set in her seat
Who later I would need in my life to complete.

Little did I know about her there
Another unique girl with stories to share
With her own past, aspirations in mind,
But in her it was my future I'd find.

Little did I know about her eyes
A deep blue color to show a spirit likewise
Eyes are the only window a soul may show
A hint of what I would learn of her so

Little did I know about her smile
Which took away all my troubles so vile
Whatever bad that was there or might be
Would go away with the smile I'd see

Little did I know what's in her past
Many love stories, and scars to last
Tales of greatness, growing, and demise,
Each page turned is another surprise.

Little did I know about her being,
Nothing else in life carries so much meaning
In her presence, I need nothing more
It plants a life fire, warmth to my core

Little did I know about her heart,
In which death I'll endure to get a part
Even just a piece, no matter how small
Nothing else in life means anything at all

Little did I know about her soul,
To know it you must get past her shoal
Much of her she keeps hidden away
To be apart of it is something I pray.

Little did I know about her love,
For all my needs this shines above
It's a deific substance in which I strive
I existed before, with it I'm alive

Little do I know about her future,
To heal wounds true love can suture,
To be a part I've earned it not
Despite the flames, amorous and hot

There's still so much of her, little I can know
Still, its in her direction I will always go
I can only wish her love, but I reserve
For deep down I know it's what I don't deserve.

Hometowne Hackettstown *by Ambrose*

If home is truly where the heart is,
Then mine is buried in Hackettstown
So deep, in fact,
That the bedrock upon which stores and houses,
Schools and banks have laid their foundations
Depend upon her for stability

True,
It's not the buildings that make the town,
But they sure do help
For Hackettstown is not the same without my parents house,
Or the old school building,
Or the M&M factory
The buildings are the accent pieces to the town,
Necessary, but not all there is to her

Hackettstown is in the people I see daily
She's in the trees that have been around for decades
And the sidewalks that haven't been level for a century
Hackettstown is in the fields where generations have played ball,
In the cemetary, which contains a multitude of histories
And most importantly, Hackettstown is in Me

Anywhere I go, she comes with me
A birthmark that never fades
She yearns to return to the soil she knows all too well
And yet, she needs the world to see her children
So that everyone may know her splendor

Even here, a short drive from her
I yearn for her always
Counting down the days, minutes, and hours
Till I may once again be within her grace
And return to my heart once more

Special Ordinary Days *by Zebulon*

It's not a special day,
But just a day
Not a special view,
But a particular view
I see it in company
But in my world I must be alone

One can just sit and observe
As one does on a day
Such as the passing car
Which contains another couple
Both simple and complex as my own

There's a certain beauty in it all,
One needs not divine inspiration
Nor quiet, nor stillness of sorts
But just eyes as they watch
And skin to feel the winds touch
The warm beating rays of sun
To be saved by the shade of true

No one's in a rush but we all are
To cram an enjoyment
Must be a relaxing matter.
It is hard work to have fun

There's nothing special of today,
Except the beaten shoreline
Rushing past and over the sand
While my love sleeps herself away

My friend escapes into a virtual world
While another friend works
A family sets off for the shore
Another departs from it

There's joy to it all, isn't there?
To be alive, to witness it all
Being a part of everyone's world
Be it the real world or our own
For we exist between characters

There's a joy in beauty so complex
Yet so simple to it all
It's not so a special day today
But it's a special day to be today!